ST. MICHAEL'S FALL

ST. MICHAEL'S FALL

RAYMOND LUCZAK

Deaf Life Press
A division of MSM Productions, Ltd.
Rochester, New York
1995

St. Michael's Fall
Copyright © 1995, Raymond Luczak.

Cover/Book Design: Matthew S. Moore
Cover Photo: Gerard Lauzon

Cataloging-in-Publication Data

Luczak, Raymond, 1965—
St. Michael's Fall/Raymond Luczak.—1st ed.

p.   cm.

ISBN: 0-9634016-8-8 (paperback)

First published in 1995

1. Poems. 2. Raymond Luczak. 3. Title.

Library of Congress Catalog Card Number: 95-83673

10 9 8 7 6 5 4 3 2
First Edition

ACKNOWLEDGEMENTS

The poems "Learning To Speak, Part I," "The Audiologist," and "Practice" first appeared in Jill Jepson's *No Walls of Stone: An Anthology of Literature by Deaf and Hard-of-Hearing Writers* (Gallaudet University Press, 1992). The poem "The Crucifixion" appeared in the author's *Eyes Of Desire: A Deaf Gay & Lesbian Reader* (Alyson Publications, 1993).

The generous support of the Poetry Society of America helped make this book possible.

From its very first draft years ago in Washington to its very last in New York, this book has been blessed by acts of generosity and faith both large and small: Sasha Alyson, Charles F. Bancroft, Jim Benham, Jim Byrne, Christine Casady, Tim Chamberlain, Richard Chenault (in memoriam), Murry Christensen, Ronnie Cohen, Ann Darr, Jack Fennell (in memoriam), Robert Giard, Marilyn Hacker, Lynn Haney, Christopher Hewitt, Mary Hoffman, William M. Hoffman, Monique Holt, Andrew Hudson, Jill Jepson, Robert La Vallie, Kenny Lerner, Linda Levitan, Gerard Lauzon, Diana Lusker, Shirley Kirshner, B.V. Marshall, J.D. McClatchy, Mona McCubbin, Lady Edwina Molesworthy, Bob Panara, André Pellerin, Dragonsani Renteria, Hugh Seidman, Marcia Steele, Frank V. Toti, Jr., Melainic Wilding, and of course my little archangel Tom.

A big flashbulb of thanks to Robert Giard and Gerard Lauzon.

I must also thank all my eight siblings for all the wonderful memories that framed my childhood.

A bountiful bouquet of crimson roses to Matthew S. Moore and his Deaf Life Press family for their continual and nourishing support through the years.

St. Michael's Church of Ironwood, Michigan, in the Upper Peninsula, was where both of my parents attended Mass, and where they eventually married. My mother graduated from St. Ambrose High School, later renamed the Ironwood Catholic School in 1968; my brothers and sisters went from kindergarten to graduation in the Ironwood Catholic school system, and we were each baptized in St. Michael's Church. The photograph, taken by Gerard Lauzon, depicts the actual demise of St. Michael's Church in 1986.

In memoriam

Anna Grzesiak
1886-1977

Edward J. Luczak
1926-1989

and

for my mother

CONTENTS

I.

Prayer to St. Michael

St. Michael, the Archangel, defend us in battle,
Be our protection against the wickedness and
*   snares of the devil;*
May God rebuke him, we humbly pray and do thou,
O Prince of heavenly host, by the power of God,
Thrust into hell Satan and all evil spirits who
Wander through the world for the ruin of souls.

THE STATUE

I.

Autumn a gathering of the brittleness to come,
muck leaves slapped the globe under her feet.
Rakes clawed at her base: Paint chips became leaves.
Weeds threatened in gusts to pass on their seeds
to gardens like ours. She listened to us playing in the house,
with 45s on the Panasonic and games off the shelves.

In winter she valiantly stood alone,
burdened with layers of snow clinging to her shoulders.
On bright January mornings from the bathroom window,
I could not pinpoint her—everything an unbroken white—
until I found her shadow of Lazarus stricken,
leaving no impression on the blank-faced scene.

Late spring rains streaked more at her blues and whites
until the true color of her plaster moldings showed.
Her pedestal did not tilt under angry sleets,
nor did she budge from the fear of slipping.
The hash-brown grasses beckoned her broken fingertips,
split infinitesimal cracks in the frozen shell of the earth.

II.

But not once did she fall of her own accord.
Once a garden sale item, she stood tall as an altar,
her manicured toes perched upon a globe
precariously balanced on an X pedestal.
Her arms hung low, her fragile palms
open and steady in her corner of the backyard.

Her veil, drawn about her body, revealed

scars of chipped plaster, now
a baby blue fading onto its core.
She was encircled with a scapular of bird droppings.
She faced the orange sun sinking west,
casting long shadows on the next dawn.

III.

Come summer I could no longer avoid her tranquillity:
Grass blades waved with dandelion whiskers, then suddenly flayed
by wind-borne whips; it seemed always the time to mow them down.
The dim garage could not contain the smell of poured gas
in the tiny tank. I rubbed lotion on my palms
so the vibrations of the mower would not dry and numb them.

Back and forth on the lawn: A shag carpet unrolled into a neat blanket,
its subtle curves exposing a pleasant revelation between sun and shade.
I plowed toward the statue: Round her base I left only tufts.
Then I bent over to hug her—she did not recoil—and almost dropped her.
My arms spasmodic from her weight, I looked at her placid face
as she lay there. Had I missed a cry of admonition, pain?

I looked around. The sky's azure had not changed.
I heaved her pedestal away to find in the grass a noodle-white X;
mowing over it, I felt good to see the tufts disappear.
With her pedestal returned to its place, I bore up the statue
but I dropped again: much too heavy even to try.
I left her there, her eyes still trusting as a child's.

A few hours later thunder clapped for rain. Standing at the toilet,
I saw, remembered: She now lay ravaged by furies of the storm.
A whiteness glowing against the dour greenery, her palms yielded
nothing. But this hideousness of forgetting tortured me,

a yearning for the same vision that sustained her so.

4

II.

"It was September 20, 1891, that history found another mark in the development in the City of Ironwood. On that date the Polish, Bohemian, and Croatian people of St. Ambrose parish formed their own parish under the patronage of St. Michael."

Ironwood Daily Globe
September 22, 1966

A SUNDAY: MAY 1972

7:30 A.M.

On Sunday mornings I was wide awake,
alert in slipping past the jam-packed beds
of Joe, David, and Mark. I eyed their heads
for sounds I'd have made; they'd jolted awake
before when I thought I was being quiet;
and stepped down the stairs. Through the kitchen's air
I glanced, tiptoed to the big bathroom where
I'd put a pile of folded clothes for flight.
My hearing aid chest harness sat on top:
pouches and a mire of elastic straps.
People thought my manners suffered a lapse
when I made the wax on my earmolds drop
off before I plugged in my ears to listen.
Once I heard my own voice, I felt christened.

7.40 A.M.

Stepping out of the bathroom, I saw Jean
and Carole yawn at the kitchen table
while Mom and Dad drank coffee to enable
them to bear chaotic epics between
eleven pairs of legs scurrying up and down
the stairs to and from dresser and bathroom.
Pajamas, socks, pants, brushes held a vroom
all their own as time approached for town.
I kept straightening my stubborn curl
with comb and water, but it would not stay.
Mark rushed in and said, "Outta my way."
I stormed off, still looking like a girl.
Why couldn't that stupid curl stay on straight?
I almost didn't care if we ran late.

9

8:11 A.M.

Crisp as peanut brittle, the air outside
sighed heavily with spring. Up on the porch
I stood, where St. Michael's spire lit a torch,
the sun striking a dime's light. To the side
I moved, to catch its precise silhouette—
or the real shape—of the silver-flamed cross.
Years before I was born, St. Michael's was
painted pink, and its mortar white: Who could forget
our church after seeing St. Ambrose or
Holy Trinity, all three blocks apart?
I stood as sparrows made a graceful dart
to sit like popcorn strung too close for
more warmth. Our house inside was a war
where everyone kept an unspoken score.

8:26 A.M.

I heaved open the big white garage door,
and peered into the dark. The double-bike
with its twin seats leaned haphazardly, like
a hippo eager to wallow some more.
I placed my shiny black shoes on the brick
floor, unevened by the soil underneath,
and through a jungle of handlebarred teeth,
I arrived at the back window for bugs to flick
with a clap of hands or a squash of my foot.
Cobwebs and grimy shadows fell about.
I wondered whether I heard someone shout.
I turned, nearly tripped over an old root.
Out of the dark I made my voyage back
and leaped to pull down the garage door: Thwack!

9:18 A.M.

Our '67 Pontiac station
wagon rolled down Oak Street as Dad's tall head
bumped against the ceiling. "All right? Your head,"
Mom asked while Dad growled in irritation.
Meanwhile, Carole pulled her finger to lips
as we made faces at our special foe—
and then Mary yelped. Mark smirked while Joe
and David poked about with elbow tips.
Andra, Kevin, and I sat way out back,
hearing all of this but watching the cars
trailing us as if we were movie stars.
If the driver smiled, we'd give a wave back.
We gabbed away nine miles a minute
although the trip to Mass seemed infinite.

9:23 A.M.

As we turned left, the Guata waved. "See you there!"
Andra giggled while Kevin fidgeted in
his synthetic V-neck sweater. His skin
felt hot when I tucked in his shirt flare.
In three weeks, summer vacation would come,
inviting us to invent some new games,
swim on Sundays, pull weeds, watch charcoal flames,
and ride bikes all day. "Andra. Mom!"
My Timex Big Ben watch from Santa Claus
said 9:25. I yelled, "We'll be late!"
Andra asked, "What time is it? Hurry!" "Wait."
I checked my watch. "9:26." A pause
before I shouted, "It's 9:26!"
The car lurched and sped off its rubber slicks.

9:28 A.M.

Carole, exasperated from sitting
between Mary and Mark, moaned, "I know!" "There!"
We pointed where Dad could park. The cool air
swept us off our feet as we tumbled out, flitting
from our wagon to McLeod Avenue.
The prickly shrubs were trimmed close to the ground,
and we tried to contain our bubbly sound,
as Mark held the glass door to let us through.
But before we went into the nave, Jean
and Mom gave us a quick lookover before
we sped to our pew. Then we hushed some more
as we lined up to the end, quite a scene.
Mrs. Pavlovich unleashed the organ
as the tall altar boys tried not to scan.

9:49 A.M.

I watched the smoke rise up to the heavens:
Burning incense made everything surreal.
I wondered why we had to sit, stand, kneel
as I sat looking around with Kevin's
sweater on my lap. I stared again at
Father Frank's lips. Him I couldn't lipread.
Instead I looked up to see myself freed
like Peter Pan, dashing without a splat,
with Tinkerbelle's bright wings sparkling his feet:
Why couldn't I? When we shook hands for peace,
we checked on everybody. I thought, Please
make the time go by faster so we can eat.
Then the congregation filled the aisle
for Communion. I slipped into file.

10:04 A.M.

Ten more minutes, *ten* more minutes—oh, Mass
seemed forever. We were primed to get out.
Time passed. Leaping up, we tried not to shout
while Mom and Dad chatted with others as
I darted out to be first at the car,
my hand already on the locked door.
At her house Grandma would show us more
of her warm molasses cookies, not far
from her hot coffee bread. She was eighty-
six, with her thin hair pinned in a flat bun
and her spotted hands waiting to press one
penny in my palm. She was a lady
who I couldn't lipread, but her eyes glowed
Sundays whenever any of us showed.

12:07 P.M.

Then we returned home. Mom donned her apron
as she joined Jean and Carole in their cooking
our meal at one. I lingered by, looking
at Jean whipping potatoes to mash. Then
Mom made the gravy, stirred both corn and peas,
and checked the pot roast. Mary placed the blue-and-white
Currier & Ives plates with forks on the right
(except for herself). Dad siphoned the grease
as Mom lifted the pot roast to its huge plate.
In the next room we watched Moe, Joe, Larry,
and Shemp poke their eyes. Finally Mary
yelled: "Dinner!" On our chairs and bench to wait,
we bowed to say grace. I held fork and spoon,
and it was never a moment too soon.

JANUARY 21, 1973

It seemed like any other Sunday except:
Father Frank lugged a slide projector
while the speaker set up the screen
in front of the communicant's stand.

I tugged at Mom's blouse.
She responded with a *shhh* on her lips.
I turned up my hearing aids.
I wondered what slides he would show.

The white glare of the projector
impaled a blindness in my eyes.
Mom motioned for me to sit
on the other side of her,

closer to the projector,
for easier lipreading.
I stared blankly at him,
trying to understand why

he had to constrain himself
with spitting words at us.
I checked my shirt for stains
as he pressed the button.

Colorful graphics showing %
and (*in Thousands*) varied
in bars, pie slices, and charts.
So many numbers. I looked up

at Mom, waiting for her to explain
all this. Tears trickled down
her cheeks, and I tried not to stare
at my brothers and sisters,

who seemed uncomfortable,
or restless like me, waiting.
I watched the colors bounce
off the movie screen to the carpet,

thick and lush with a somber red.
Suddenly it turned a stark crimson.
The slide showed a photograph
of an eight-week-old fetus,

its blood staining a gray sheet.
"Mom." She shook her head, *No.
Not now.* "Mom. . . ." I stared,
my throat as dry as my eyes.

The speaker pressed his button
for more until I almost closed my eyes.
But I kept my eyes open.
I was afraid to miss something

I could read on his lips.
"Pray to God. . .write letters. . .
so many. . . ." That was all
I could catch. Later that night

I dreamed a sharp
iridescence of blood
casting its steady beam
on the carpet, its silence.

JULY 4, 1974

We stripped quickly down to swimsuits and dove like
baby dolphins: Star Lake was so clear that one
   day on the white sands.

Chills reverberated with us gasping, "Oh!—it's
cold!" Our thighs showed goosebumps, their faint hairs on end.
   We strayed in further,

past the chill: Our knees shook, toes wriggled. "Look! Look."
We pointed, sometimes answered with splashes. "Hey! Not
   fair!" And Dad panned his

movie camera from a picnic table,
calling us to wave for him, but we dove in,
   fugitives hiding.

But we couldn't stay underwater for long—
so we shot like rockets, our flat bangs heavy with
   water. We shook our

heads as we plodded back to shore, our bodies
shivering under towels while Mom pointed to
   noses, ears dripping.

After eating hot dogs and chips, we squeezed in
our hot station wagon. We read the arrows
   home for our fireworks.

* * *

Joe was the first to leap out the car, inserting
Mom's keys in the doorlock, and running upstairs.
                    Shades were down, casting

golden gloom where he took out his firecrackers,
Roman candles, twirlers and matches. Mom and
                    Dad waited out front

on the porch steps, from where St. Michael's could be
seen, its silver cross quiet as the sun dropped west.
                    Dad gave out boxes—

shiny sparklers!—while we watched Joe, Mark, David,
Paul and Randy light, one after another,
                    bricks of firecrackers,

rockets in Coke bottles, and squealing spinners.
Dusk felt sweeter when Mr. Lewinski called
                    from up the street to

cut the racket. We shrugged while Joe fixed a
different way to light a firecracker under
                    discarded hubcaps.

Then the fireworks beyond St. Michael's started.
Nice, but we agreed ours were more exciting,
                    something like Star Lake.

DIALOGUE I: MAY 1975

"Mrs. Chambers, what is a Jew?"
The dinner table had been cleared,
with gravy dripping to the bottom
of the dishwasher while the boy,
aged nine, waited for her answer.
"A Jew is someone who doesn't believe

Jesus was the Messiah. They believe
he will come. Besides, Jesus was a Jew."
He mused for a while her answer
as she wet her washcloth to clear
the table of its crumbs. The boy
then pointed to the table's bottom

where the dog Ace wagged happily his bottom
for more. "But I thought everyone believed
in Jesus." She smiled at the boy.
"The world has many religions. Jews,
Catholics, Buddhists—" The word wasn't clear
to him, so she clarified her answer:

"They believe God is not the answer
to everything, but peace comes from the bottom
of their own souls. Is that clear?"
"But what happens if they don't believe
in Jesus or God? You know, the Jew
people." She looked at him. "Boy,

you ask the hardest questions!" The boy
blushed, but he listened to her answer.
"You don't call them the Jew
people—the Jew*ish* people." Ace's bottom
stopped when she wiped her hands. "They believe
in heaven like we do." The boy's clear

gray eyes hesitated. "No, I wasn't clear
enough. . . ." To the dining room window the boy
followed her. "We must respect what beliefs
other people have." Her finger then answered,
pointing to a copper dome near the bottom
of the valley. "That's where the Jews

pray and believe." Ace rested his bottom
while the boy said nothing to her answer:
Things were not so clear for him or the Jews.

III.

"... . the parish joined with the Holy Trinity to build a grade school and convent for the Dominican Sisters from Oxford, Mich., who had taught catechism in the two parishes beginning in 1943."

Our Sunday Visitor
September 25, 1966

THE SISTERS AT ICGS

Sister Virgene, *1972*

You were the first nun I'd met. Your pointed and
black glasses, rapid and eager smiles during
         lessons for First Communion on
      Saturday afternoons with Mom at

a distance: Your index finger showed where I
should read. I liked the colorful pictures of
         Jesus and Mary, so I read out
      loud while you smiled at my nasal words from

the page. I looked at Mom who'd also smiled, and
continued until we had to leave. You waved
         bye-bye when I zipped up my jacket,
      eager to go home and play with Kevin.

Then came the month of May: I sat in second
row, staring at Father Frank whose opaque eyes
         unnerved me. I turned my head, saw my
      family, waved to them, but Carole's eyes

and finger pointed back to Father Frank. Then
I stayed in line, not sure if this was
         connected with those pictures of
      Jesus and Mary. I mumbled, "Amen,"

swallowed my host, and walked back to my pew while
grown-ups lined up for their turns up front. Then I
         saw you, your face serene as you winked
      down at me. I knew I'd done the right thing.

Sister Regina, *1976*

What was the answer to the big question of
those bland flowers? You explained the mystery
    of pistils: How they gave life to the
    seeds that must dig into the ground of

their mothers. I took notes in my Science notebook,
carefully tracing the skeleton of the
    generic flower: filament, style,
    ovary, stamen, and anther. What did

it mean, to know the flower? God's universe
struck me odd, strange: Why must the flower bloom and
    wilt? Couldn't it stand up forever?
    It was fall when you explained how seasons

affected flowers, trees, and the river
nearby. I stared outside the windows and
    remembered dandelions dying,
    how Dad made wine from their flat yellow heads.

What was your answer? That Sirius, the Dog
Star, twinkled because God loved us? Your eyebrows
    frowned when I lost trail of your thoughts.
    I never asked: Never learned your answer.

Sister Anne, *1977*

Enunciating words for the spelling tests:
Your wide lips showed your teeth as you stretched them out
in case I couldn't understand you.
I scribbled them down, my eyes on yours as

you spoke the next word. I cringed from thinking how
my class would snicker at how she moved her lips
LIKE THIS. I prayed they would not come to
me, their lips WIDE and CLEAR. They thought it real

funny when I couldn't understand their words.
"B.J." "What?" "You know, B.J.!" They shook their heads
at me while I stood, wondering what
it meant. I knew it must be a dirty

word —why else would they laugh so hard at me?—
but I was too afraid to ask them or even you.
I didn't know where to turn, or how to
spell it. I spelled my silence perfectly.

SWING

pull your shorts down some
so your skin won't gasp

when you sit on the hot
black rubber sling

braid your pinky fingers
into the slightly rusty chains

jump and drop your legs for the sun,
a magnifying glass on your eyes

squeeze your eyelids shut
as you fall backwards

let your stomach flip
as dustclouds powder your bangs

your tenners toe together,
a pair of sparrow wingtips

now bend your legs, oars
for the breezy waters

open your eyes now
everything is purple-white

you blink behind eyelids
photographic negatives

your shoulders lean forward,
past your flint-edged fingernails

a dandelion whisker locks
suddenly in your nose

you brush it off as
you hold your breath

ready for a dive,
a zip through rain

a swoop over the pothole where
the dirt shows your Bigfoots

reach again for the sun,
bright as yolk

you contract into a doll,
your legs now stiff

you look above your head
as your shadow freezes

a rock poised
in a slingshot pouch

your shadow balloons
as your toes barely touch

a dustcloud rises
as you squint at the sun

one day you will fly there,
just close your eyes

THE AUDIOLOGIST

The thick gray windows never reveal
her shadowy figure. The audiologist
always has something to conceal
behind those windows. She only reveals
to Mom how I did this year. I steal
a look at my audiogram and her checklist.
The thick gray windows never reveal
her shadowy figure: The audiologist

and I are at war
over my ears, my headphones, my chair.
First she makes a beep, or a low roar—
and then I'm at war
with myself. Did I truly hear
that or not? My hand shoots up in the air,
volleying against her score
over my ears, my headphones, my chair.

The thick walls absorb my silence.
I cannot hear anything from outside,
except through my ear-burning, tense
headphones. They absorb her silence.
I wrestle with my ears, my conscience,
as I close my eyes to listen, decide.
The thick walls absorb my silence
as her sounds come from the other side.

LENT 1977

The snow finally fell away to slush,
gray glops that splattered heavily on knees
when cars sped around corners in a rush.
I couldn't wait to kick my boots off, sneeze
and peel down my pants for another pair,
where I could feel my cold dryness. Sometimes
I'd hold my clammy toes near the hot air
vent linked from the furnace downstairs. My eyes
caught the bleak white landscape across the street:
St. Michael's stood a dull pink above trees,
their branches void of buds. I thought of sweets,
how I'd given them up. I was not pleased.
There had to be a legit way to buy
them—M&Ms?—from Hulstrom's on the sly.

Near cash registers and parking meters,
I kept my eye out for lost change in stores.
I hid the mine of coppers and silvers
under my pile of shirts, growing with more
pennies until I had about fifty
cents three weeks later. That dry Saturday
I carried books back to the library,
checked out the Hardy Boys shelf, took away
a few upstairs where Mrs. Peterson
would stamp due dates with a half-glassed smile.
Once on the granite steps I leaped and ran
down one block on Aurora Street. With style
I quickly broke into a saunter south
on Suffolk Street. How my tongue filled my mouth. . . .

I stayed left, careful to survey the front
windows of Hulstrom's; I stopped to look
at the glassed display of Leather Goods, daunted
by wondering if the Hulstrom's salesclerk
was Catholic, and whether she'd tattle
on me? I fingered my money until
they turned warm from my contemplation. Hell,
I thought, trying to sound reckless with will,
and crossed the street. The slush looked a swamp
as I almost misstepped, but I was quick!
Now past the typewriter store, I felt damp
with sweat. I looked both ways before—one blink!—
I stepped inside. *Ironwood Daily Globe*
and the other papers I gave brief probes.

I scanned as usual the magazine rows,
taking in cellophaned X-rated mags,
or what I could glean from what they could show.
Their lurid colors glared, hitting a snag
of fear: What if they saw me staring near
Newsweek, *Esquire,* and *Time?* I turned away
past *Mad* and *Spy vs. Spy* paperbacks
to where candies lay in profuse display.
I eyed the salesclerk as she turned her back
to tap her Marlboros, just leaning near
the Slush Puppy Machine and tourist maps
of Ironwood and Copper Peak, before
I gazed elsewhere: back to licorice snaps.
My eyes swept outside the storefront once more.

Darting back and forth between Tootsie Rolls,
Red Swizzles, Twix Bars, Peppermint Patties,
Lemon Drops, and Pez, my throat lost control
of speech. Instead, my finger showed what pleased:
Mounds Bars, green Dynamints, and Reese's Cups.
Meanwhile, I glanced elsewhere, my hand taking
out forty-five cents as shown on her screen.
She smiled faintly when at last I looked up
to take my tiny bag. No one had seen
my entrance; no one would catch my leaving.
Inside my hands inside my mittens were wet with sweat.
I glanced around for any passing cars.
I stuffed my loot into my coatpockets.
Then I thought no, and pulled out my Mounds Bar.

As I glanced past Hiawatha's statue,
I chomped away on the forgotten taste
of coconut and chocolate. It felt new
in my mouth; I wondered: Why must I wait
another week and half before Easter?
I wolfed down Reese's Cups in seconds flat,
afraid a passing car would see me eat
like Jesse James. Eating peanut butter—
well, somehow it felt flat, no longer sweet.
Because: I was condemned to Hell, that's what!
I climbed the heavy snowbanks and sought clean
snow. Taking off my mittens, I shoved some
into my mouth, its melting a sharp freeze.
I moved my books to my other arm: Home.

THE SEASON OF FUR

Frosty's brown-black nose
showed one freckle
on one nostril.
His wet, black lips
panted hot breaths
on our laps
for scraps off our plates.

Winters he slept
coiled, a spiral
of Siberian Husky.

His bushy tail
pulled curtains
from his nose,
warm and safe
from the snow fallen
the night before.

Summers his fur
turned a brown-white.
Rain turned his yard
into cushions of mud.

In the shade
of his doghouse
we bent down
to dig tugging
fingers
into that thick fur
behind his hind legs
and plucked fists.
We opened them:
cotton balls on the wind.

We stared
at his freshly white spots
and felt the sticky film
of hairs on our palms.

He sniffed the winds
as we plucked more,
and more,
until he turned
white, scrawny, young
again.

TWO LITANIES: OCTOBER 1977

I.

Mom, I thought of you in the two days you'd disappeared.
Your sudden absence in the house was unspeakable,
throwing me into a quandary of questions:
What's a stroke? What did Jean mean, Grandma
can't talk no more? By early afternoon
you knew she had died; you slipped

away into her now-crowded house, slip-
ping into hugs of those who appeared.
That rain-soaked afternoon
when I came home from school, an unspeakable
fear tainted my thoughts of Grandma:
Dead? It seemed impossible, what with questions

of having just seen her that Sunday. Your question
of her death was answered with buying her a new slip,
dress, and shoes, and leaving again to choose Grandma's
casket. The gloom over here disappeared,
if only for a while, when you came home late, unspeaking
from exhaustion. I waited all that afternoon,

wondering whether I'd get to ask you. That afternoon
I kept asking Andra questions:
But the look on everyone's faces was unspeakable.
I felt I'd somehow slipped
in my understanding. I wanted to disappear
from not feeling the same way: I had to see Grandma,

but they all said, No, I'd have to wait for Grandma
at the wake. I tried to read Hardy Boys that afternoon,
but there was no mention of death, only disappear-
ances. I turned up my hearing aids for questions,
but their answers seemed to slip
out of my earmolds, remaining unspeakable.

I watched you, wanted to talk, but an unspeakable
heaviness hung on your shoulders. I wished Grandma
would just sit in Dad's chair and watch me slip
in my socks across the smooth kitchen floor all afternoon,
just so I wouldn't need to ask all those questions.
I wondered about the two days you'd disappeared,

unspeakably not there in the gray afternoon.
I imagined Grandma nodding at my questions
until the moment you quietly reappeared.

II.

Grandma, I stared at your crossed arms
surrounded by white lilies, white roses
and white envelopes. I felt somehow harmed,

the scent of your silence striking my nose.
It chafed through the fragrances.
Self-conscious in my kneeling pose,

I tried my best not to elicit glances
whenever my knees shifted their weight.
I wondered about your embalmed trance:

Your face was never a pallid white.
But everyone said you looked good.
Hearing that filled me with fright.

Chappell-Zielinski Funeral Home in Ironwood
was packed with people who hadn't seen
you for years. They did what they could,

didn't Dad say so? Your sleep seemed
so fake, unreal. I stared at your crossed arms,
debating a whisper: something like "It's me."
I wondered if you'd come to any more harm.

IV.

"Do not the most moving moments of our lives find us all without words?"

Marcel Marceau

CROSSROADS

The long sharp incline that led onto the boulevard,
a Y in a banana split: one end toward St. Michael's,
the other toward our home on Oak Street.
The black pavement smoothed upward at 50 degrees,
a lasting impression with no potholes.

In that Summer of the Skateboard, our Zeus
flattened into gnarled plastic and urethane wheels,
I rode back and forth on the kitchen floor. Safety
held my precarious hands above stove and doorframe.
Arching high above the pads—a pair of talons on wheels—
the blue skateboard was not mine, but my brother Joe's.
All scratched and gashed, it leaned easily with my weight.

The day the roadworkers took away the sawhorses,
all of us kids trooped up through that August evening.
Joe had long since found a megaboard; but I carried
his battered blue board. It weighed
somehow heavier in my palms, now a sooty sweat
from black sandpaper adhesives on top.

Joe went down first: His guts were innate.
He had snared a dead skunk, aimed sharp rocks
with his super-duper slingshot at glass bells
atop telephone poles, and stole grins in Mass.
A poised statue on wheels, he was already our Icarus.
A string of taut statues followed.

The view daunted: Downtown Ironwood lay below our right,
with St. Michael's silver cross deflecting the sunset rays.
Cars came from both directions on the boulevard,
that awkward stem with bruised fences bridging cave-ins.
Lives had been lost, here and there, in these shut mines.

The few left behind eyed me, already thirteen,
then cast my face aside from their thoughts. I sat positioned
myself on Joe's board. My tenners fitted together.
With whitened knuckles on the board's sides,
unable to think of checking behind me, or even to decide
which of the two roads I should lean toward,
I let fly. Now: the crossroads.

SPELLING BEE 1978

A giddiness overtook my entire
soul when Jeanine misspelled. I knew
the word: T-I-M-B-U-K-T-U.
My ears and my eyes were taut as a wire,
zipping between Sister Priscilla and
my class for clues to the next word on her
lips. I'd given up TV night after
night, searching words I didn't understand
and memorizing them. I had to hide
away, I imagined how they would sound,
so in the basement I spoke them out loud
and prayed they'd pronounce the same way as I. . . .
The day had come: Now Jeanine shook her head
and groaned as I turned gleeful in my dread.

Michelle, Lee Ann, and I stood near the door
while everyone watched the teacher's pencil
check off words already used. She was still
on the second list, I knew not much more
was left: She'd followed more or less what I'd
remembered from my lists. But sometimes she'd
abruptly pick from a new list. Then feed-
back squealed more from my hearing aids when I'd
tried to hear her better, but that was what
I feared most, those looks as if I should
have been *prepared*, and she'd done all she could
to help me understand the next word. "What?"
Her face tightened: No, I didn't deserve
those privileged repeats. I hated her nerve.

As I watched Michelle, and then Lee Ann, spell
their words correctly, I thought of The Friend
sitting behind Greg's desk. Among the "friends"
in my class, he'd given me the most hell:
He laughed when he saw how I couldn't play
with his dog-chewed green Nerf football. He knew
I'd wanted friends, but he never cared to
say hello. I hoped. But he looked away,
slapped fives with his new friends, and nudged Tony
and Greg at me. I stood under the eaves
as I stared the puddles filled with brown leaves.
I imagined bumps of potholes only
tiny islands expecting coconut
trees and warm winds. There was always a but. . . .

I discovered, when I turned off my aids
and watched The Friend assert basketball rules,
I felt less lonely in not feeling fooled
with everything, in sweet silence, that made
a playground. Standing by myself, I dreamed
of being buddies with The Friend. We'd ride
our bikes all over Ironwood; he'd cry
out whoops as he dared to drop low and lean,
now slowing down around corners downtown.
We'd snicker with a look when old ladies
jumped back to let us by. We'd see movies
and lurk together in alleys downtown.
That nothingness in my hearing aids was
sweeter in somehow softening his loss.

Now in the classroom, he drew my weird face.
I ignored him as Sister Priscilla
gave me another glance—that Attila
the Hun look—as she repeated the phrase.
"What?" I racked my brains—what did it sound most
like? I mouthed to myself the word, not sure
what I was saying. The Friend looked assured,
his not-again glances striking the coast
of faces looking back at me. Would I
make it? "It's a thing?" "—Yes." "Where is it in?"
"—You know the rules." Pages of the list in
my head stayed picture-perfect in my eyes.
"How many syllables?" She said it as
I sought for clues in the eyes of my class.

They revealed nothing, but I counted three
syllables: Was it in my memory?
"Sa. . .lack . . .tight?" "We don't have any
more time." She didn't move, she looked at me.
"I don't know—S-A-L-A-C-K-T-
I-T-E?" "Close!" I watched her on the board:
STALACTITE. I thought how Mom had explored
those dark caverns once, before she had me:
"Why didn't you say Kentucky?" My ears
burned when I realized I'd just talked back to
Sister Priscilla! Her face turned hard. "—You
sit down, Ray, and we'll all finish up here."
I did so while The Friend tugged at his ears
for me. I bled quietly in laughter's fear.

TRAINING BRA

My hearing aid harness hid
my electric breasts under my shirt.
Once the boys saw how I changed
batteries in class, they snickered.

At recess they said, "It's a bra.
Where's your boobs?"
They gestured triple-E cups
and slapped fives.

The next morning I reached for
my socks in the dryer.
I felt a strap of my sister's bra.
My fingers on fire, I burned.

CONCERTO

In Grandma's house, Mom's upright piano
sat with a metronome. Unhooked, it sprang to life,
expecting my fingers to follow always
those ticks. The weight of the metronome
rocked quickly, or languidly, depending on where
I set the tempo—my hearing aids

picked it up easily. I drank some Kool-Aid
as my brother David poked a bit at the piano
and then ambled out to the garage where
the lawn mower was. At last alone, I came to life;
I peered through the side windows, set the metronome,
and cracked my knuckles. I thought, I'd always

do this if I played in Carnegie Hall. And, always,
I made sure I'd jacked up my body aids
to hear more of my playing than the metronome:
Sharp sounds always cut better than the piano.
My right foot felt for the pedal, and then my secret life
as Beethoven began. . . . My fingers tiptoed over where

soft notes would ting, as a prelude. Somewhere
around the corner David was mowing, always
neatly in squares. I heard his engine's life,
loud and quiet, and then loud and quiet. My aids
were close enough for the pedaled echoes of the piano,
even with the dull-minded metronome.

Oh, I tried so hard to keep rhythm with the metronome!
It ticked the same no matter how or where
my fingertips strayed on the piano. . . .
So I surrendered to that urge, as always,
to just play *sturm und drang* into my body aids,
my eyes closed and my fingers sweating with life.

Then I stopped abruptly—what a life,
holding my clawed fingers in mid-air! The metronome
ticked twice before I attacked again. Then my body aids
squealed with feedback; I turned them down until where
it stopped. I became Beethoven again, always
longing for a better audience than myself at the piano:

They'd always applaud my life's passion on the piano
instead of that metronome. And of course my hearing aids
never caught David's tiptoes—*boo!* My fans scattered elsewhere.

SUMMER NIGHTS 1979

The green light of our Panasonic stereo
flickered whenever one of us turned the dial.
I dreamed of being cool, like Disco,

so I turned up my hearing aids. "Do you know
this one?" Sometimes it took Andra a while:
The green light of our Panasonic stereo

blinked. "Mary! How does this song go?"
But the chorus provided soon enough the title.
I dreamed of being cool like Disco

as I lay under the living room window
with my body aids next to the speaker. While
the green light of our Panasonic stereo

stayed awake, Donna Summer sang "Heaven Knows."
I danced alone, trying out John Travolta's style.
I dreamed of being cool like Disco,

rainbow suspenders, and 8-track tapes. I'd show
off by dancing smoothly or dressing real wild.
The green light of our Panasonic stereo

made my sweaty and peach-fuzzy legs glow
in the Hustle: mere steps to my new style!
I dreamed. . . . Being cool like Disco

I wrote poems, using titles off the radio.
I felt glorious! But someone always changed the dial,
the green light of our Panasonic stereo,
my dreams of being cool like Disco.

PRACTICE

I stared at the black telephone
in Grandma's house
a bike ride from home

The receiver drooped like a brick
as I watched the slow wheel
whir back into place to "0"
after each number I dialed

In the dining room
I held it upside down
near my body aids

Exposed for the occasion

I stared at the kitchen
almost warped linoleum floor
a yellowing white

And waited
a loud ring then three ripples

Then a man's voice said hello

Hello
      Hello?
                      I stared
at the lid of holes
choked with brown dust

This is is Ray

Oh Ray Raymond This is Dad

I squinted at the smooth tear
under Grandma's old chair

      Dad

Yes yes You understand me
This is so great
How are you doing over there

I wondered what kind of things
would he say on the telephone

It's hot here

He laughed It's hot here too

        I never heard his laugh so
        close in my ears

Ray You ready for your word

Yeah

Okay here we go Superman

What

Superman

I closed my eyes What

Superman Su per man

What

Superman Su per man Superman You know
It's a bird It's a plane It's Superman

It's a word I know that

      Superman Can you understand me

I thought No why do I have to practice

What is it now

      It's Superman It starts with a S

Stupid man That's not one word That's two words

No Ray Listen Listen now Superman
He's from the comics

The receiver turned hot in my hand
fingers bleeding with sweat

I don't understand Dad

No Try one more time Superman Su per man
He flies like Peter Pan

Duperman beaterman That doesn't sound like a word

Super man Superman Ray

I stared at the cradle

    Well I I can't understand you

    OK Bye bye now

I wished

My body aids alone
on the kitchen floor
smash

    Smash it
with the receiver

V.

"That man's silence is wonderful to listen to."

Thomas Hardy
Under The Greenwood Tree

LEARNING TO SPEAK, PART I

Mary Hoffman, didn't you know what you had
done when you drove all the way from Ramsay, those
gray photocopies stacked up beside you in
your car?
        Your long blonde
hair, thin fingers, a tiny waist and eyes that
lit up at how I'd imitated signs off
your hands as we turned the sheet over for the
next sign, an arrow
indicating how I should whoosh right through the
air, my palms flat like airplane wings and yet so
coordinated with my mind, buffeted by
seeing Ironwood's
only deaf man, Gramps.

                    He worked evenings at
Hurley's Holiday Inn, in its kitchen, where
he was dishwasher. Afternoons he sat in
front of the bar near
Santini's Gift Shoppe, his hands folded on his
lap, until one kid or two came with their hands
fingerspelling their names or something until
he smiled, or laughed. He
would then fingerspell, slowly, so that they could
understand it. I stared at his lips, hardly
moving.

        I thought how I hated my voice, the
faces all the kids
in my class made when I tried to explain what
I had meant: Why couldn't I just sit there like
him, not having to say anything? I sneaked
into the public

library and found some old sign language books.
I took them home, hiding them in my Jacquart's
burlap bookbag and reading them upstairs where
no one would catch me
trying arrows, wriggles, and stillness on the
bed. Sometimes I'd hear quite suddenly the click
of the downstairs door opening—I'd slam my
book shut and cover
it with something else so no one would ever
think I was learning to be Gramps in secret.
And I rather liked the blue Deaf-Mute Cards he'd passed
out. One found its way
home: our kitchen table. I picked it up, piqued:
Who was that man, smiling with ears sticking out?
"My name. . .GRAMPS, a Deaf-Mute. . .Thank you so much for
your kindness." Handshapes
showed how A to Z could be formed; I wondered
how this contraband piece was smuggled in, and
left just so, with Mom kneading dough right next to
it. I stared, thinking:

> *Does it mean I'm allowed to learn?* I learned it
> anyway. The handshapes fit so easily,
> perfectly. It got so I practiced running
> through everyone I
> knew until their names felt natural on my
> fingers.
> Late at night I dreamed of a voiceless
> world, where everyone signed and understood me.
> Lipreading would be
> banished, or at least, expectations of me
> having to lipread. I longed to be more deaf,
> mute like Gramps who sat in front of Hulstrom's and
> waved when I sped by
> on my ten-speed bicycle.

                                                   I wanted to
stop, to see his eyes take me in with my
earmolds sticking out like his ears too under
his baseball cap. I
wanted not to have to say anything, to
isolate myself from the rest of them, the
boys who laughed at my nasal speech, Father
K's silent gazes,
and the teacher's apologetic looks. Well,
if I couldn't hear as well as they, I thought:
Might as well learn.

                              So Mom told me right then,
that you would come in our
house to teach me what you knew. They seemed resigned,
as if they knew I would learn it anyway.
You came frequently, and then you called Mom to
apologize, I
can't come today. She told me later you had
multiple sclerosis. I couldn't see you
in my mind: your fingers stiff, unable to. . . ?

But the next time you
came, you only said, Sorry, I was sick, and
opened to where we'd stopped the last time. Then
came the day I *knew*, that I wouldn't see you
again, not for a
long time.
                    Later I took to riding into
town and seeking Gramps on his bench. I parked my
bike beside where he sat, and talked for some time.
We fingerspelled to
each other as passersby shook their heads at
us, *deaf people*: Look how they can talk without
voices!

Mary Hoffman, didn't you know what
you had begun when
you agreed to teach me my first, and then the
next sign, until I couldn't stop, not until
I became Gramps, not mute but raging instead,
hands howling volumes?

HUMMINGBIRDS

Our new Sheet Metal teacher left
us boys alone in the cafeteria.

> *My notebook was filled*
> *with sugarcubes of want*

One of them said, "Hey you!
What you doin' over there?"

> *My fingers were only*
> *hummingbirds in a small cage*

I sat up and freed
my deaf voice, my hearing hands

> *They fluttered under my chin,*
> *in front of my chest, everywhere*

The boys' eyes narrowed like a cat's
for a minute. Then they stood up.

> *My voice faltered as I felt*
> *their fierce wings beating*

"Fairy! Look at his hands
swishing in the air!"

> *Lilacs' fragrances melted*
> *under globs of solder*

The boys flaunted limp wrists.
I shot all my birds in mid-flight.

DIALOGUE II: MARCH 1981

One night when I fell asleep, I dreamed what
could be done to create for them boys hell:
Their own eardrums would be popped if I won.
I woke up at six-thirty, left house at
seven, walked to the back of St. Michael's,
donned my cassock and surplice. I was done. . . .
But the weekday Mass hadn't started yet.
I stared at Father K reading Thomas
Aquinas—was it More?—in his grim pose.
I took my chair next to our coats, all wet
from mists hanging low on gray slush. He was
quiet, saying nothing as he changed his clothes
to kiss the amice before wrapping it
around his alb. I wondered: Is that it?

This much I'd grasped: When I first went in there
after my brother Joe to serve my first Mass,
Father K smiled at me as I searched for
a pair of buckled shoes that would fit. Where
was size seven in there? I became cross,
and nervous, when size eight had to do for
now. I matched the Velcro patches in front
of my cassock; wrestled with the surplice.
They both shook their heads while Joe showed me how to
slip gangly arms through its sleeves. "Now, just don't
worry about it," Joe said. "It's not as
hard as you think." He opened curtains to
let all of us through the sanctuary.
I followed Joe; Father K followed me.

As I kept Joe's pace, I felt my loose shoes
clucking against the back of my feet. I
knew my ears were now pink with my freckles
as we walked past the mostly empty pews;
on weekdays not many people came by.
I kept my eyes on back of Joe's freckled
neck while the bleak light from the mosaic
windows cast a shine on the smooth pews. I
square-turned left, and again to the front where
the altar stood. Joe planted the cross back
where he'd taken it, and took his place by
Father K. Then we both sat on our chairs
as Father K went to his lectern and
gave all the sign of the cross with his hand.

I sat, my eyes blankly centered on where
no one sat. I felt safe, not seeing eyes
I'd surely recognize if I saw them
looking back. They held the prayerful stare
on him: I finally saw that much, my
blank eyes casting furtively about him
and them. I also caught Joe's look that said,
Stay cool. I thought of how small my feet felt
inside those shoes, and wondered how many
boys had worn them. Then itches on my head
got worse. Should I scratch them? I'd surely melt
if Father K caught me. Minutes—how many
more? It seemed like hours, even though I
was watching the balcony clock tick by.

Then came the moment, what we were there for:
To pass the cruets of water and wine
to Father K, nodding distractedly
as we returned to the side with finger
towel and dish. He blessed His Blood, divine.
We stood at a distance, the Mystery
of waiting before holding the brass plates
under their chins. I tried not to quaver
in holding my plate while their tongues held out
to receive with Amens. I had to wait
for years until Father K said prayers
to end the Mass. Father K looked about
but we were ready, genuflecting. He
followed after us to the sacristy.

Having seen close the motions Father K
made, I'd turned quiet as Joe laughed at my shoes,
its noise of clucking. I put on my coat,
hoping Father K would send Joe away.
As he led us out, Father K smiled. "Joe's
one hell of a guy." He buttoned his coat
as I stared at Joe shrugging. Past Carlson's
delivery doors, we walked to our school.
Joe said nothing. How I fumed, hating him
joking with Father K about nonsense;
what, I couldn't understand. I'm a fool,
I thought, to have said yes to serving him
when Carole brought it up. But the next day
I went on with Joe to serve anyway.

So while Father K resumed reading his
book, I thought at last a *good* hard question
for him. "Father. . . . If God made the world, who
made God?" He looked up and fixed his glasses,
drilling through me. "God, of course." I questioned
still: "But *who* made God Himself?" "God, that's Who.
It's one of those things you must have faith in."
He smiled, and then went back to his book. That
moment I felt the bricks up high shudder
before they landed at my feet, fallen
in dust. The taste of St. Michael's stayed flat
as Father K kept reading. I wondered,
but not for long, whether he'd tighten his
cincture as I picked lint off my surplice.

VI.

"An Ironwood landmark met its demise this morning. The spire of St. Michael's Catholic Church was the last remnant of the building to fall before Centennial Construction demolition equipment."

Ironwood Daily Globe
December 17, 1986

THE CRUCIFIXION

I was only an innocent boy at the time.
My parents tried to explain to me
what the word "crucifixion" meant,
but I could not lipread them.
As I trailed after them for Jerusalem,
they chatted amiably with each other,
and met a caravan of speech
therapists who chatted amiably too.
They frowned on every gesture I made
when I tried to speak more clearly.
My voice was not good enough. I turned
my hearing aids, but all I heard was
their seamless chatter.

Ravens leaped from their olive trees,
wings spreading wide for the winds.
They were also coming to Jerusalem.
My parents always covered their ears
when they let out a series of caw-caws.
I loved them because they were so *loud*.
And their wings! They were a joy to watch,
their chest-beating show of power.
Some distance behind us there were people
laughing and pointing at the ravens.
They did not talk, but their bodies sang
with their hands: the most beautiful caw-caw.

My parents saw them too, and promptly turned me
around to the front. I imagined
speech therapists whispering to them:
He must learn to speak right. I practiced
my *st*'s, *r*'s, and *w*'s with fervor.
They clapped hands whenever I got them right.
You're saved from those barbarian hands.
My parents' eyes had never been so full of relief
they almost cried. Over the last hill before
Jerusalem, I saw the smooth mound of Calvary Hill
rising high. While my parents pointed at it,
I stole a glance back at those weird people.
They must be gypsies, I thought. There,
an older man winked at me, his gnarly hands
gesturing I should throw away my hearing aids.
I riveted my eyes back to the road.
My father tousled my hair,
for I now knew better than to stare;
he'd said gypsies always kidnapped children
like me, and they never saw their parents again.

As I scampered down the dusty road, I tripped
and knocked a boy down. Our hearing aids clashed
like jolts of volts: We got up and looked
at each other. I pointed to his hearing aid,
wondering why he had one when I had two.
He pointed to his empty ear and shook his head.
He turned abruptly still when our parents stood
behind us. I looked up at the angry faces
of our speech therapists. My mother compared notes
with my friend's mother while we hungered
after each other's hands. Finally—and

suddenly—my father said, "We mustn't be late."
We hurried on, before the gypsies could come
close. They became quiet when they recognized
our speech therapists surrounding
the two of us. I gave them a smile:
Their hands flurried suddenly into wings.
We doubled our pace, and so gained quick
admission into the city. I looked behind
and saw the gates closing on them.
My friend and I looked at each other, suddenly lost.

Huge ravens alighted on the eaves of roofs
and clotheslines bouying on the wind. My caravan
melted into the crowd's clamor for the death
of Laurent Clerc, the gypsy who'd claimed to be
the king of us all. As we pushed our way closer,
the road became covered with broken shrapnel pieces
of hearing aids. They smoked like burnt cinders.
My parents didn't even notice, they were too busy
chanting. I looked around and caught a woman
whose mouthing didn't fit in with the crowd's chants.
Then I saw there were many of *them*, mouthing
without a sound. My friend's eyes also blinked:
There were gypsies right in our midst!

The crowd's electricity changed when the Roman
soldiers shoved to clear the way for Clerc.
I bent low and followed my friend to the forefront
where we could see him better. There he was:
dragging along a cross made of piano boards.
Sweat dripped from his chubby body,
soaking his loincloth of a hearing aid harness.

His double chin sagged from awkward speech,
his throat swelled from a thousand therapists' hands,
his naked feet bled from the sharp metallic cinders.
Right behind his heels was King Alexander Graham Bell.
I quaked in his stern presence, his long gray beard
flapping in the wind. Ravens stretched their claws
back and forth while they circled above him.
I watched King Bell flay Clerc's crisscrossed back
with a whip of piano strings, and saw his eyes glow
when he saw how Clerc couldn't speak. His hands
were wild with rage, trying to let go his cross.
I saw a thousand tears in the eyes of disguised gypsies.
King Bell whipped him again, and again,
proclaiming, "You must speak! You must speak!"
The crowds picked up on this, chanting along.
Clerc fell at last, his face now ruptured by the sharp
edges of broken hearing aids. I broke out of
the crowd and slid the cross off his back.
Clerc's eyes spoke with tender thanks
as King Bell stared at my hearing aid harness.

"How dare you do this to him? He doesn't deserve
your pity." I tried to answer,
but the words came out all wrong. He drummed
his fingers on his elbow as I tried again,
and again. He smiled whenever I got a word
right, and said, "Good. Say it again, but remember
to make your *t*'s clearer." The crowd turned
enormously silent as I spoke slowly:
"You. . .don't. . .have. . .to. . .hurt. . .people."
They clapped furiously while King Bell hugged me
and shouted, "See? He speaks so well!

This boy will be my heir." He tousled my hair
as he beckoned me to step aside. I watched him
brandish his whip before Clerc twitched again.
Bits of hearing aids dug into his flesh.
King Bell kicked his sides until Clerc turned over.
He bent down and said slowly into his face,
"Do you understand what this boy said? He said,
'You don't have to hurt people.' That's a lot
more intelligent than you could say with hands!"

Clerc took a deep sigh and heaved himself up.
His eyes locked on mine as he mouthed slowly
so I could lipread. His gestures said:
You like talk? Your-hands easy—
King Bell whupped his hands short.
"I understood every sign you made!"
The crowd turned to watch his queen Mabel's hands fly:
It's true, he's right— "No." He looked
around, and signed very bluntly *something*.
It looked like a whip. Her face dropped, grim.
King Bell ordered his soldiers to haul the cross
back on Clerc's shoulders. As I watched the two
dissolve into the following crowds on Calvary Hill,
I felt a man's hand stroke my shoulders softly.
He had to be one of *them*. I followed him
through a maze of alleys to a tiny room upstairs.
The windows were covered with burlap curtains
as he lit a candle. The room burst into gypsies
surrounding my friend, who had no harness on.
He was the happiest boy I had ever seen.
They imitated animals and all sorts of people,
and he laughed. I couldn't help it either,
and found our fingers groping for their signs.

Later that day we stole our way toward Calvary Hill.
Alice Cogswell's face looked sad as she prayed
nearby until she recognized one of us. Her face
lit up with unspeakable joy as she looked around
to make sure no one was watching our hands
flickering near our waists, away from our faces.
Babies future same again never. Proud my teacher.
We nodded, not looking directly into Clerc's face
while his flabby arms sagged on the cross. We tried
not to feel the rusty nails staked in the heart
of his hands. *Say last words couldn't.* I looked
into her eyes, hardly silenced with rage.
I watched the bored gazes of King Bell's guards
before I said, *I-f he-can't, many-many future-will say
last words his.* The gypsies tried not to appear
too excited as they led me out of the city. Ravens
swooped playfully all over us, caw-cawing noisily.
As I walked past the front steps of the king's temple,
I noticed the frantic footsteps of speech therapists
paid to convince parents teaching Speech was the Way,
the Only Way into the larger world. After I'd left
Jerusalem, I looked back on Calvary Hill.
Clerc's cross was no longer a shadow looming starkly
in the evening sun. Outstretched hands reached instead
higher into the sky, and they were all our own.

LEARNING TO SPEAK, PART II

Oh yes: I learned how to speak.
Shuttling between speech therapists, I had no choice,
for everyone I saw could speak
like people on TV. I watched them speak
slowly, I took in their lips with my eyes,
and then I *had* to speak:
I mumbled, not always sure how to pronounce. "Speak
up louder!—What?—I don't understand
you." I cleared my throat. "You don't understand?"
I nodded and looked away. Yes, I'd learned to speak,
pretending not to feel the shame over my voice;
truth was, I hated using my voice.

I listened to my speech therapist's voice
with my headphones, and then mine, when I had to speak—
repeat the words off her projector with my voice.
She said, "Oh good good!" when my voice
echoed in that drafty classroom. What choice
did I have? I wanted home, in Ironwood, for Mom's voice
and Dad's thick hands. Sometimes I couldn't give voice
to anything, I floundered and just cried. My eyes
felt so blurry, strained from feeling their eyes
on me as I tried to listen to my own voice.
How could they understand
that speech was hardly what I wanted to understand?

What I really wanted to understand
was why I had to work, work, work on my voice?
I found that so hard to understand.
Kids were out there, playing. They could understand
me, couldn't they? I could speak
clearly enough, couldn't I? I just couldn't understand

why me, why I had to understand
how the tongue could curl, or hold, for a choice
of vowels and consonants. I never had a choice—
the kids out there didn't have to understand
how. "Now do it again." I watched their eyes,
one speech therapist after another. I eyed
their reactions whenever I spoke. My eyes
took in everything else I needed to understand:
their cold fingers on my throat, their arched eye-
brows and their notes jotted under my eyes.
"You must repeat each word after me with your voice."
Then came that moment of judgment in their eyes
when I hesitated. I wanted to shield my eyes
from theirs, not having to hear them speak
of how I could do better. Why must I speak?
Alone, I listened with my eyes.
At least I had a choice,
nothing like my speech therapist's lack of choice.

I wrestled with my tongue her choice
of consonants—I liked vowels, *i* as in "eye"
or *a* as in "play"—but that was never her choice.
Sometimes I sat there, plucking a choice
daydream, more pleasing to my eye
than a mimeographed list of choice
words: I would be everybody's choice
for Best Friend in spite of my voice.
They would understand my voice
anyway and agree with my choice
of not having to speak.
But I had to, even if I didn't want to speak.

Why, I've asked myself all these years, why speak?
Cold fingers on my throat gave me no choice:
I fitted my earmolding tears under my eyes
when I came to understand
why I had this peculiar voice.

CANARIES

My hands are canaries,
pairs of wings fluttering
from one branch of language
to another, together
in portable cages of space.

How they await hidden
on perches for their next cue
to chirp freely. They adore
the peace of motions.
And they have the best yellow

wings.

DECEMBER 17, 1986

I didn't weep at all when I learned
about Bishop Schmitt, and how no one could earn
enough money to save St. Michael's Church
from the wrecking ball's lurch.
(I'd told Mom and Dad that God's Word
was no longer among my concerns.)

A few days later I had heard
from Mom how they took apart the church.
I didn't weep.

Then she sent me the *Daily Globe* pictures
of the wrecking ball. The grid,
the spire of St. Michael's stood naked. I searched
for the familiar details of my church
while somewhere in my heart I lurched.

The pink bricks: Those I finally discerned.
This time I wept.

VII.

"It will be seen that the world a deaf man inhabits is not one of complete silence, which is perhaps the chief complaints he has to make about it. The world in which I live seldom *appears* silent. Silence is not absence of sound but of movement."

David Wright
Deafness

MONTREAL RIVER

for my father 1926-1989

Four blocks away from Wisconsin: I grew
accustomed to the border dividing my Michigan from the other side.
The shallow waters slithered like an uneven snake,
its intestines swarming with tadpoles in cool shade,
its circulation carrying the occasional Dairy Queen sundae bowl.
Insects thrived under weeping willow trees hanging
their leafy clothes on lines just so
over the river. I leaned
many times, always searching for something beyond my knees.
What was I looking for?
I forgot now: Perhaps a daydream left behind
with my missal at St. Michael's had suggested this. Wading
then, I moved slowly with my eyes locked on
ever-flickering shards of Budweiser bottles flung on the rocks.
Leaves sped by like cars
in front of my house, carrying downstream mosquitoes standing,
calmly and safely as on a raft. How nice that would feel,
secure in the knowledge of survival. The mottled branches filtered
   white light
from the afternoon sun; I peered through the river's opacity:
Velvet simmered with the unknown, the shards.

Once, the summer before, I stepped on glass but it cut not so deep.
The wound let out blood tinting a darkness to all that flowed.
I stood there, shaking my foot over the waters and watching it drip
over the gelatinous motion until I dipped it in again to cleanse
   the wound. Now I stared
for what seemed hours into the ceaseless motions rolling over
rocks that barely pierced the surface. It was a cape,
a shimmering satin that never touched anything but gave air to
   everything.

Underneath my feet were awkward stones, but not as many
as in Lake Superior. It was not as cold
but not deep enough to submerge myself into the motions threatening
        to carry me further
away from the shores, from any chance of salvation. I'd be no longer
        in my own hands,
but in the hands of God. That meant I'd have to pray harder,
make fervent promises that somehow were never fulfilled once I
        recovered.

In that flint-eyed winter I climbed over the snowbanks
to where the motions hid. It was all ice,
a thick plastic wrap marked by wrinkles. I stared down at it,
but silence met my eyes: No motion at all. I climbed back
up and broke free a stiff branch, and thrashed it on
the ice. No motion, just scratches through the thin layer
of snow. I banged my boots on it; a bubble burped as
it hit the ice's sole. I pushed down a little
and again, waiting for a break. Finally, a crack: The water seeped out.
In the fading sun it appeared a luminous gray,
lit by the streetlamp over the parking lot nearby. I sat back and stared,
        smiling. The river held a life away
from having to listen all the time for strange and familiar sounds:
The river was so easy to listen to.
One only had to sit and watch.

ABOUT THE AUTHOR

Raymond Luczak lost much of his hearing at seven months due to double pneumonia, but his deafness was not diagnosed until he was two years old. After graduating from Gallaudet University in Washington, DC, he moved to New York City in 1988. His play *Snooty* won first place in the New York Deaf Theater's 1990 Sam Edwards Deaf Playwrights Competition; the plays he has written since have been produced all over Manhattan. He edited the anthology *Eyes Of Desire: A Deaf Gay & Lesbian Reader*, which garnered two 1993 Lambda Literary Award nominations. Stories from his much anticipated novel *Loud Hands* and other poems have appeared in numerous anthologies, including *Men On Men 4*. A frequent contributor for *CTN Magazine*, he makes his home happily in Manhattan.

Also available from
MSM Productions, Ltd./Deaf Life Press

★ **DEAF LIFE.** $30 for 12 issues (1 year); $26.00 prepaid. ISSN 0898-719X.

The Deaf Community's #1 magazine. This independent monthly began publication in 1988. Entertaining, informative, and educational, with high visual appeal. Contains profiles of newsmakers and achievers, coverage of politics, law, sports, education, media, the arts, technology, events, and controversial issues. For all readers—hearing *and* deaf.

★ **FOR HEARING PEOPLE ONLY: Answers to some of the most commonly asked questions about the Deaf community, its culture, and the "Deaf Reality."** By Matthew S. Moore and Linda Levitan. With a foreword by Harlan Lane. Illustrated by Robert L. Johnson. Paper, $19.95 (ISBN 0-9634016-1-0). Hardcover, $35.00 (ISBN 0-9634016-2-9).

An innovative "Deaf Studies" handbook, written in a simple, clear, non-technical style, for those without *any* prior background. Here in one handy volume—in a Q&A format—are concise answers to some of the most commonly asked questions about deaf people, deaf/hearing issues, sign language, and communication. All 60 installments of the popular "For Hearing People Only" feature from the first 5 years of **DEAF LIFE** are included—fully revised and expanded. Each chapter illustrated.

★ **Meeting Halfway in American Sign Language: A Common Ground for Effective Communication Among Deaf and Hearing People,** by Bernard Bragg and Jack R. Olson. Photography by Denise Stenzel. Edited by Donald F. Moores. With a foreword by Merv Garretson. Hardcover, $39.95. ISBN 0-9634016-7-X.

This is a textbook for hearing people who are *not* fluent in sign language but want to be able to communicate successfully with Deaf people. A "user-friendly" approach to an old problem. More than 2,000 photos accompany the text, making this the most lavishly-illustrated photographic sign-language book ever published. An ideal supplementary text for intermediate sign-language classes—but can be used and enjoyed by beginning and advanced students as well.

★ **Great Deaf Americans: The Second Edition**. By Matthew S. Moore and Robert F. Panara. with a foreword by Dr. Yerker Andersson. Illustrated. Paper, $24.95. ISBN 0-9634016-6-1.

Newly-revised, expanded, and updated. Over 5 dozen brief biographical profiles of eminent deaf people in a variety of fields, from aviation to teaching, representing the diversity of deaf identities in America, from culturally-Deaf to oral, from born-deaf to late-deafened. Each chapter illustrated with full-page portraits or photographs.

★ **Victory Week**. Text by Walter P. Kelley. Illustrations by Tony Landon McGregor. Hardcover with dustjacket, $18.95. ISBN 0-9634016-9-6.

Tony L. McGregor's gorgeous watercolors highlight this child's-eye view of the "Deaf President Now" uprising at Gallaudet University in March 1988. A major event in the history of the U.S. Deaf community, simply retold for children. Fully illustrated in color; oversized format.

For more information, contact: MSM Productions, Ltd.,
P.O. Box 23380, Rochester, NY 14620-2405.
FAX: (716) 442-6371; TTY: (716) 442-6370.